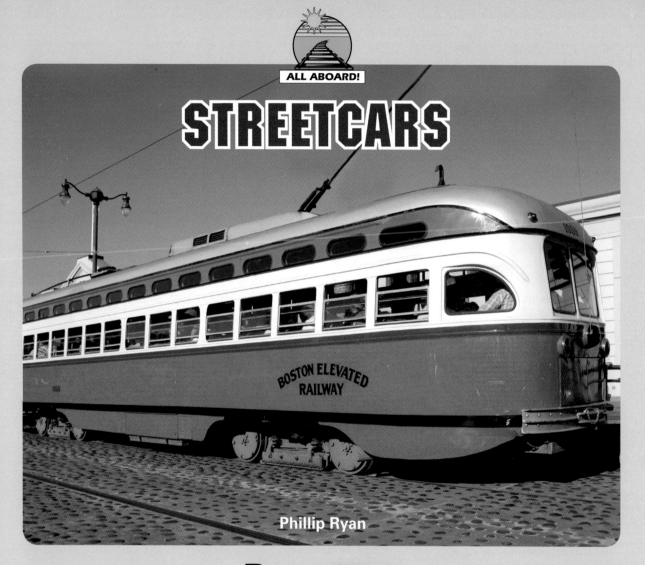

ALL ABOARD!

STREETCARS

BOSTON ELEVATED
RAILWAY

Phillip Ryan

PowerKiDS
press™

New York

Published in 2011 by The Rosen Publishing Group, Inc.
29 East 21st Street, New York, NY 10010

First Edition

Editor: Joanne Randolph
Book Design: Ashley Burrell
Photo Researcher: Jessica Gerweck

Photo Credits: Cover, p. 17 Shutterstock.com; p. 5 Glow Images/Getty Images; pp. 6–7, 9 Walter Bibikow/Getty Images; pp. 10–11 Hisham Ibrahim/Getty Images; p. 13 © Sylvain Grandadam/age fotostock; p. 15 © Jean-Marc Charles/age fotostock; pp. 18–19 George Rose/Getty Images; p. 21 Medioimages/Photodisc/Getty Images; p. 23 Travel Ink/Getty Images.

Library of Congress Cataloging-in-Publication Data
Ryan, Phillip.
  Streetcars / Phillip Ryan. — 1st ed.
    p. cm. — (All aboard!)
  Includes index.
  ISBN 978-1-4488-0639-3 (library binding) — ISBN 978-1-4488-1219-6 (pbk.) — ISBN 978-1-4488-1220-2 (6-pack)
  1. Street-railroads—Juvenile literature. I. Title.
  TF148.R938 2011
  625.6'6—dc22
                                        2009050918

Manufactured in the United States of America

CPSIA Compliance Information: Batch #WS10PK: For Further Information contact Rosen Publishing, New York, New York at 1-800-237-9932

CONTENTS

Have you ever heard of streetcars? Streetcars can also be called trolleys or trams.

Streetcars are small trains. They often run on or next to streets.

Streetcars get their power from an overhead **wire**. Do you see the wire here?

Streetcars run on **tracks**. The tracks are set into the ground.

Streetcars are driven by a person called a **conductor**. This person sits at the front of the car.

Streetcars carry people. They pick the people up at the **station**.

4204

⚡ FGV

15

Sometimes a streetcar has only one car. It can be cheaper for a city to use trains with one car.

Some streetcars have more than one car. This one has two cars.

18

Some cities use old-fashioned streetcars. They may do this to remember the past.

POWELL
AND
MARKET

13

HYDE AND BEACH
FISHERMANS
WHARF

Streetcars can be a fun way to get around the city!

WORDS TO KNOW

conductor

 station

tracks

 wire

INDEX

WEB SITES

Due to the changing nature of Internet links, PowerKids Press has developed an online list of Web sites related to the subject of this book. This site is updated regularly. Please use this link to access the list:
www.powerkidslinks.com/allabrd/lrt/